Why do People Eat?

Kate Needham

Designed by Lindy Dark and Non Figg
Illustrated by Annabel Spenceley and Kuo Kang Chen

Revised by Philippa Wingate
Cover design by Russell Punter
Cover illustration by Christyan Fox
With thanks to Katarina Dragoslavić
Consultant: Dr. Frank Slattery and Valerie Micheau

CONTENTS

Why do you need food?

Your body is like a big machine that is always working. Even when you are asleep your heart is beating, your lungs are breathing and your brain is working. Food is the fuel which keeps all these things going. Without it you would slow down and eventually grind to a halt.

An apple gives you enough energy to cycle for six minutes.

People need food just as cars need fuel.

A bar of chocolate gives you enough energy to walk for an hour.

Growing big and strong

People sometimes say you have to eat things to grow big and strong. This is true because your whole body is made from good things in the food you eat.

Until you are about 18 your body is growing all the time.

Measure yourself each month to see how quickly you grow.

Sometimes when you haven't eaten you feel weak. This is because your body is running out of energy.

Children who don't get enough food stop growing. They become thin and weak and fall ill more easily.

Too much

If you eat more food than your body needs you store it as fat. This makes you heavy and slows you down.

Some people want to be big and heavy so they overeat on purpose. For example Japanese sumo wrestlers need to be heavy to fight.

Sumo wrestlers look like this.

On the mend

The good things in the food you eat help your body make repairs if it gets damaged. They also help you get better when you are ill.

When you cut yourself the food you eat helps your body to mend quickly.

Water

Water is what keeps your body moist and makes your blood flow around. Without it your body would dry out and stop working.

You can last several weeks without food but only a few days without water.

Loading and unloading bread from an oven is hot, thirsty work.

Shipwrecked sailors more often die of thirst than hunger, since they can't drink sea water.

People who work in hot places, such as a baker, need to drink more because they lose water when they sweat.

What is food made of?

Everything you eat is made up of lots of different things called nutrients. These are the good things that keep your body going. Proteins, fats and carbohydrates are all nutrients. Each one helps your body do a special job.

Protein

Proteins are like building blocks. Your body uses them to grow and repair itself. Different kinds of protein help build up each part of your body.

Pregnant women need extra protein to help their baby grow.

A mother's milk has special protein in it.

Proteins build up muscles and make your hair grow.

Teenagers use up lots of protein because they are growing fast.

Meat, eggs, fish and cheese have lots of protein.

4

Carbohydrate

Carbohydrates give you energy. You need energy for everything you do, such as running around, talking, thinking, even reading this book.

You get lots of energy from sweet things but it doesn't last very long. The energy you get from pasta, cereal or bread is better because it lasts longer.

Climbers often carry a bar of chocolate in case they need extra energy in an emergency.

Sporty people need carbohydrate for extra energy.

Bread, cereal, pasta and cakes have lots of carbohydrate.

Fat

Fat also gives you energy but unless your body needs it right away, it is stored in a layer around your body. This acts like an extra piece of clothing helping to keep you warm and protect you.

Butter, margarine and oil are almost all fat.

Fat stored on your bottom makes it more comfortable to sit on, like a cushion.

What else is in food?

The food you eat also has tiny amounts of nutrients called vitamins and minerals which you need.

What do vitamins do?

Vitamins are like little workers which help other nutrients to do their jobs. There are about 20 different kinds. Most are named after letters of the alphabet.

The chart opposite shows what some vitamins do and where you find them.

A

Vitamin A helps you to see in the dark.

You find it in egg yolks, liver, full fat milk and carrots.

B

There are lots of kinds of B vitamins, each with a different job.

Cereals, dairy products and meat have B vitamins.

C

Vitamin C is good for health and body repairs.

You find it in fresh fruit and vegetables.

D

Vitamin D helps make your bones and teeth strong.

You get it from eggs, fish and butter.

Sailors used to get scurvy – a disease which stops wounds from healing. This is because they were at sea for months without any fresh vegetables or fruit and so no vitamin C.

Your body can make vitamin D itself using sunlight. People who live in less sunny countries need extra vitamin D from their food.

6

What are minerals?

Minerals are nutrients that plants get from the soil and pass on to you. You need about 15 different ones, such as salt, calcium and iron.

Water has lots of minerals in it.

Milk, cheese and yogurt have calcium in them which makes your teeth and bones strong.

Liver, meat and spinach have tiny amounts of iron in them which you need for your blood.

What is fibre?

Fibre is the tough bit of food that you don't digest. It helps carry food through you and takes waste out the other end.

Brown bread, cereals and vegetables have lots of fibre.

If you don't eat enough fibre you get constipated – this is when you can't go to the toilet for ages.

What do you eat?

Write down everything you ate and drank in your last main meal. Then see if you can find out which nutrients each thing has. Use the last two pages for help.

roast chicken - protein
potatoes - carbohydrate
vitamin C
peas and carrots -vitamin A
vitamin C
fibre
strawberries- vitamin C
ice cream- nothing
particularly
good

How many good things did you eat? Were there any you didn't get any of? Some things you eat, such as ice cream, may not have anything particularly good in them, see page 16.

7

Where does food go to?

When you eat, your food starts a long journey through your body which takes about three days. It travels through a tube called the alimentary canal which starts at your mouth and finishes at your bottom.

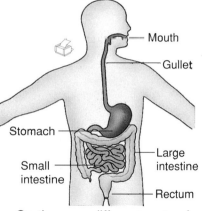

Mouth
Gullet
Stomach
Large intestine
Small intestine
Rectum

On the way, different parts of your body work on the food and add juices with chemicals in them. This breaks food into microscopically small pieces that can go into your blood. This journey is called digestion.

Food's journey
The road in this picture is like the alimentary canal, and the men show what happens to your food.

Your mouth

These men are like your teeth, cutting food into tiny pieces.

The water is like saliva. It makes food soft and mushy.

Your tongue rolls the food into a ball and pushes it into your gullet, like these men with brooms.

Your gullet

Then you swallow, and food is carried off from your mouth to continue its journey.

 Internet link For a link to a website where you can learn more about your food's journey through your body, go to **www.usborne-quicklinks.com**

How long to chew?

The smaller food gets in your mouth, the easier it is for your stomach to work on. Tough meat or food with lots of fibre needs more chewing.

Eat a mouthful of apple. Then eat one of cheese.

See how many times you chew each one before you swallow.

What makes you choke?

Your gullet is next to your windpipe (the pipe you breathe through). When you swallow, your windpipe closes to stop food from going into it.

If it doesn't close in time your food might go down the wrong way. This makes you choke which usually sends the food back again.

Windpipe

Gullet

Your stomach

To your intestines

In your body, it goes off down a tube called a gullet. This delivers food to your stomach by squeezing it along.

Your stomach is like a big mixing machine. It churns your food up until it is like soup.

Your stomach stretches to hold enough food to last you several hours. Turn the page to see what happens in the intestines, where food is pushed to next.

Good things and waste

After about three hours the soupy mixture in your stomach moves on to your intestines. There, all the good things in food are taken into the blood. The way it happens is called absorption. Waste moves on to leave your body. This is the longest part of food's journey.

How goodness is absorbed

The walls of your small intestine are so thin that the nutrients in your food can pass through them.

The nutrients go into your blood and are carried around your body.

Tiny folds stick out of the walls of the small intestine.

Blood flows all around the folds, ready to carry off nutrients.

Goodness

Waste

Your small intestine

First the food arrives in your small intestine. This isn't really small at all, as it's a long tube all curled up.

As the soupy mixture passes through it, more juices are added. Then nutrients are absorbed into your blood (the man's sign tells them to stay). The rest goes into your large intestine (the man's sign tells them they must go).

Your large intestine

Your large intestine is fatter than the small intestine and it's nearly as long.

Some water and salts go into your blood from here, like this water down the drain. The rest is waste.

Getting rid of waste

Waste from your large intestine is solid. It goes into your rectum and is pushed out through your bottom.

Waste water is turned into urine in your kidneys. It is stored in your bladder until you go to the toilet.

Kidneys

Bladder

Rectum

Anus

What makes you burp?

When you eat you often swallow air with your food. Sometimes your body sends the air back up through your mouth. This is called a burp.

Burp!

Eating too fast makes you swallow lots of air and so you may burp.

Food poisoning

If you eat food that is bad, your body tries to get rid of it quickly.

Your stomach muscles may push it back up your gullet. This is when you are sick.

It may rush through you and come out the other end as diarrhoea.

Internet link For a link to a website where you can find out more about why we burp, go to **www.usborne-quicklinks.com**

Keeping food fresh

Your food is also food for tiny living things called microbes. These can make fresh food go bad after a few days. If you want food to keep you have to stop microbes from getting at it. They like moisture, warmth and air, so food kept in cold, dry places with no air lasts longer.

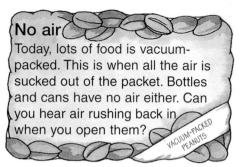

No air

Today, lots of food is vacuum-packed. This is when all the air is sucked out of the packet. Bottles and cans have no air either. Can you hear air rushing back in when you open them?

VACUUM-PACKED PEANUTS

Keeping food cold

Cooling food slows microbes down: freezing it stops them altogether. Today, food can be kept in refrigerators or freezers until it is needed.

Cold cellars have been used to keep food for centuries.

The cold does not kill microbes, so you still have to eat food quickly when you defrost it.

Drying food

Drying food gets rid of all the moisture so microbes can't multiply.

Grapes are dried to make raisins, sultanas and currants.

Today, food can be freeze-dried. This is when it is frozen and dried at the same time to get rid of moisture. You add water when you eat it.

Astronauts use freeze-dried food as it's light and takes up little room.

Heating food up

Cooking, sterilization and pasteurization are all ways of killing microbes by heat.

Sterilized food is heated to a very high temperature to kill all the microbes. It lasts a long time.

Vinegar in pickles

Sugar in jam

Salt in bacon

Food in cans and bottles is sterilized.

Preservatives: Benzoic acid (E210)

Preservatives

Preservatives are chemicals that make food last. Natural ones like sugar, vinegar and salt, have been used for centuries.

Look at labels on cans to see what other chemicals are used as preservatives today.

Pasteurized milk is heated enough to kill dangerous microbes. It lasts a few days.

Before pasteurization, cows were led around towns and milked on the doorstep.

Food from far away

These days food can be kept fresh for so long that shops have exotic fruits from all over the world. They travel in special refrigerated ships.

Next time you go to a supermarket, see if it says where the fruit comes from on the shelves.

Pineapple

Mangoes

Banana Passion fruit
Lychees

Food you store loses some nutrients, particularly vitamins, so it is better to eat fresh food.

13

What makes you hungry?

When your body needs food, it sends a message to your brain to say so. Then you look around to find something to eat.

Sometimes, when you can see or smell food you like, it can make you feel hungry even though your body doesn't need food.

Nose smells food

Eyes see food

The smell of food tells you if it is good or bad and if you like it or not.

Even thinking about food can make you hungry.

Stomach is empty

What makes your mouth water?

When you see or smell food you like, your body gets ready to eat. You may feel water in your mouth. This is saliva, the juice your mouth makes to help you mix your food.

Saliva dripping from a dog's mouth means that he is ready to eat.

Tummy rumbles

Sometimes, when your stomach is getting ready for food it makes a rumbling noise. The sound you can hear is air and digestive juices being pushed around inside.

Internet link For a link to a website where you can explore your sense of taste and smell online, go to **www.usborne-quicklinks.com**

Tasting food

You can tell what food you do and do not like by the taste of it. Your tongue is what you mainly use to taste food. It is covered with lots of tiny bumps called taste buds.

Look closely at your tongue in the mirror to see your taste buds.

Bitter

Sour

Salty

Sweet

There are four types of taste buds. Each tells a different kind of taste: salty, sweet, sour and bitter. They are on different parts of your tongue.

The smell of things helps you taste them as well. Try holding your nose when you eat. Can you taste your food?

Try this

Dip your finger in some salt. Put it on the tip of your tongue, then on the back and finally on the side. Which part can you taste it on the most?

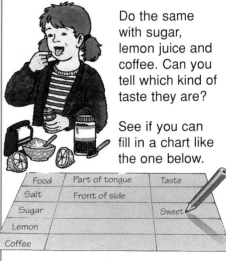

Do the same with sugar, lemon juice and coffee. Can you tell which kind of taste they are?

See if you can fill in a chart like the one below.

Food	Part of tongue	Taste
Salt	Front of side	
Sugar		Sweet
Lemon		
Coffee		

Professional tasters

Some people can tell different tastes more easily than others. They may become professional wine- or tea-tasters

Internet link For a link to a website where you can find out all about your taste buds and just how much you use your tongue, go to **www.usborne-quicklinks.com**

15

Food that's bad for you

If you only ate your favourite food, your body wouldn't get all the good things it needs.

Some foods have very little goodness and can be bad for you if you eat too much of them.

Sweet things

Sugar is what makes things sweet. It is a carbohydrate, so it gives you energy, but too much of it makes you fat. It also makes your teeth rot.

The more sweet things you eat, the more fillings you are likely to have at the dentist's.

Fatty food

Food that is fried, such as a burger, has lots of extra fat. It makes you feel full so you may not eat other things that are good for you.

Having extra fat is like carrying heavy bags. Your body and heart have to work harder to carry the weight.

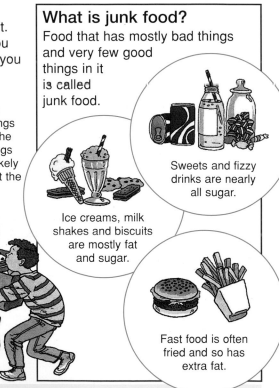

What is junk food?

Food that has mostly bad things and very few good things in it is called junk food.

Sweets and fizzy drinks are nearly all sugar.

Ice creams, milk shakes and biscuits are mostly fat and sugar.

Fast food is often fried and so has extra fat.

Internet link For a link to a website where you can see a food pyramid showing how much of different types of food you should eat, go to **www.usborne-quicklinks.com**

What is a food allergy?

Some people feel bad every time they eat a certain kind of food. They may get a headache or a rash or be sick. This is called a food allergy.

One person's favourite food can make another person feel really ill.

Quite a lot of people are allergic to fish, eggs, strawberries or shellfish.

Special problems with food

Some people's bodies can't store sugar so they only eat a little of it. Some need injections to help their bodies use sugar properly. This is called diabetes.

Some chocolate is made with less sugar, and people with diabetes can enjoy it too.

Other people's bodies don't like gluten – a protein in wheat. They can't eat things with wheat or wheat flour in them. This problem is called coeliac disease.

Can you guess which things in this picture have wheat in them? The answer is on page 24.

Religion

Some people don't eat certain kinds of food because their religion says they shouldn't. Muslims and Jews don't eat pork for example.

Where does food come from?

Almost everything you eat comes from a living thing: either a plant or an animal.

Bread and cereals come from corn.

Beef, cheese and milk come from cows.

Plants make their own food, using energy from the sun. Animals eat plants or other animals. So do people. The way one thing eats another is called a food chain.

Energy from the sun

You get energy from cow's milk.

Energy goes from the grass to the cow.

In this picture, do you know where all the picnic food comes from? Can you find out what the food chain of the egg is? Turn to the bottom of page 24 for the answer.

People who don't eat meat

People who choose not to eat any meat are called vegetarians. Some don't like to kill animals and think the way they are kept is cruel.

Some people don't eat anything that comes from animals. They are called vegans.

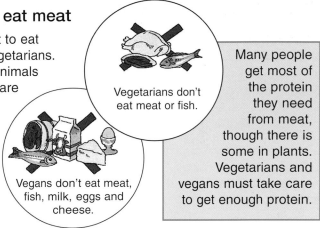

Vegetarians don't eat meat or fish.

Vegans don't eat meat, fish, milk, eggs and cheese.

Many people get most of the protein they need from meat, though there is some in plants. Vegetarians and vegans must take care to get enough protein.

How are animals kept?

For most farmers it is more important to produce lots of food cheaply than it is to give an animal a nice life. This is because people usually buy cheaper food.

For example, hens usually stop laying eggs at night. But if they are kept in warm cages with the lights on, they lay for longer.

Hens that run around the farm are called free-range hens.

Hens kept in cages are called battery hens. They can lay about 270 eggs a year.

A free-range hen may only lay 80 eggs a year, so its eggs are more expensive.

Is there enough food?

If all the food in the world was spread evenly among all the people, everyone would have enough to eat. But it isn't like that.

In rich parts of the world like Europe, North America and Australia, most people get plenty to eat. Some eat too much.

Families in rich countries tend to be smaller so there are fewer people to share the food.

In poor parts of the world like Africa, South East Asia and South America people have a lot less to eat. Many don't get enough.

Families in these countries tend to be larger so there are more mouths to feed.

Other problems in poor countries

Without rain you cannot grow things. Some African countries have had no rain for several years and their farmland is now desert.

If there is a war, land for growing food may be destroyed. Often food from other countries can't get through to help feed people.

What is malnutrition?

Malnutrition is when people don't get enough of the right nutrients. This means they catch diseases more easily.

In many poor countries people don't get enough protein. Children especially need protein to grow. Most protein comes from animals. They are expensive so many people can't afford them.

What is a famine?

A famine is when there is so little food that people die. Often they die from diseases caused by malnutrition.

Who helps?

There are organizations in rich countries which send some food to help the places where there is famine.

Future food

If the population of the whole world keeps growing there won't be enough food for everyone, particularly meat, fish and eggs.

So scientists are busy searching for new kinds of food, especially plants with lots of protein.

Soya is a plant from China which has lots of protein. It can be made to look and taste like other food.

Some seaweeds are rich in protein. They grow all over the world but are only eaten in a few countries, such as Japan.

Around the world

People in different countries eat different things. This is because each part of the world has different plants and animals. This map shows you three main crops that grow in different parts of the world.

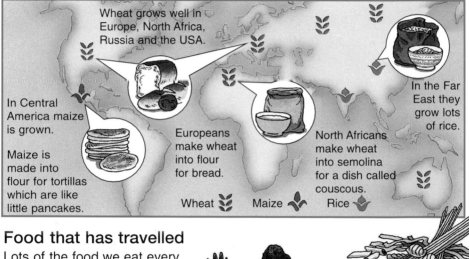

Wheat grows well in Europe, North Africa, Russia and the USA.

In Central America maize is grown.

Maize is made into flour for tortillas which are like little pancakes.

Europeans make wheat into flour for bread.

North Africans make wheat into semolina for a dish called couscous.

In the Far East they grow lots of rice.

Wheat   Maize   Rice

Food that has travelled

Lots of the food we eat every day originally came from distant countries.

In the 16th century, Spanish soldiers brought back potatoes from South America.

Turkeys were first found in Mexico.

Spices like cloves, pepper and cinnamon were carried from the East in the Middle Ages.

A famous Italian explorer, Marco Polo, brought pasta from the Far East.

Internet links

For links to more websites about food and nutrition, go to the Usborne Quicklinks Website at **www.usborne-quicklinks.com** and click on the number of the website you want to visit.

Website 1 – Meet the members of the Vita-Men team, and find out how vitamins help your body to fight disease.

Website 2 – Browse a friendly online guide packed with fascinating facts about food, where it comes from, how it's made and some of the problems concerning modern food processing.

Website 3 – Here you'll find information about the dangers of overeating and under-eating.

Website 4 – Choose from a wide selection of healthy and delicious recipes for breakfast, snacks and main meals.

Website 5 – Take a tour through the story of milk and find out everything you ever wanted to know about it.

Website 6 – It's a good idea to eat five servings of fruit or vegetables every day. This site tells you some fun ways of making sure you eat healthily, and has a chart you can print out to keep track of what you've eaten.

Website 7 – Learn about nutrition and making healthy food choices with animations and games.

Website 8 – Find out how to build a healthy body on this fun website, with puzzles, quizzes and a virtual milkshake maker.

Index

First published in 2001 by Usborne Publishing Ltd., Usborne House, 83-85 Saffron Hill, London EC1N 8RT, England. **www.usborne.com**